LIFEGUARD

Beach First Responder

Dr. Peter R. Chambers
Illustrated by Santy Gutierrez

ISBN: 978-1-943258-83-3

Published by Warren Publishing
Charlotte, NC
www.warrenpublishing.net
Printed in the United States

To Mom and Dad, thank you for instilling a love and respect for the ocean.

There are lots of people who protect and keep you safe, Firefighters, Police Officers and Sheriffs, EMS and Park Rangers.

But there is one first responder you don't think about.

The LIFEGUARDS.

Sometimes they work for Ocean Rescue, Marine Safety or the Park Service. They can be part of the Fire Department or Law Enforcement.

No matter who they work for, the lifeguard is someone who keeps you safe in, on and around the ocean or open water.

Lifeguards have lots of responsibility, training and equipment ...

but their MAIN job is to prevent
accidents, keep you safe and rescue
you if you get in trouble in the water.

They provide emergency medical care.

They rescue people from cliffs.

They respond in boats.

They help kids and adults who are lost,

and animals who are in trouble.

They patrol the beaches.

Lifeguards run special programs called,
"Jr. Guards," it's a blast!

Lifeguards also help people with special needs have fun at the beach and try new activities with special equipment and programs.

Did you know that lifeguards
do all of these things?

Remember the lifeguard wants you
safe and to have fun soooooo ...

www.nmblf.org

All proceeds of this book will go to the
North Myrtle Beach Lifeguard Foundation,
a not for profit 501(c) (3) corporation
operating exclusively for charitable purposes,
specifically to promote beach safety and ocean rescue.

ACKNOWLEDGMENTS

Thank you to the following for their commitment to beach safety:

- The Department of Ocean Rescue North Myrtle Beach Public Safety.
- The United States Lifesaving Association (USLA) leadership-past, present, and future.
- Pam Menaker, whose commitment made this book possible.

ABOUT THE AUTHOR

Peter R. Chambers, PhD, DO
a.k.a. "Surf Doc"

When not in the water, Dr. Chambers is an emergency room physician. He is an open water lifeguard and serves as the medical director with the North Myrtle Beach Ocean Rescue in North Myrtle Beach, South Carolina. He is a true waterman, and a proud United States Air Force Veteran/Flight Surgeon.

Surf Doc's motto is to always
"SWIM NEAR A LIFEGUARD".

CPSIA information can be obtained
at www.ICGtesting.com
Printed in the USA
BVHW061055010323
659483BV00002B/57

9 781943 258833